D1085320

KRISHNA AND THE MYSTERY OF THE STOLEN CALVES

KRISHNA AND THE MYSTERY OF THE STOLEN CALVES

Joshua M. Greene

ILLUSTRATIONS BY
Dominique Amendola

KERSHAW COUNTY LIBRARY
632 W. DeKalb St. Suite 109
Camden SC 29020

INSIGHT KIDS
A MANDALA BOOK
San Rafael, California

*L*ong ago, in a cowherd village called Vrindavan, there lived a child who did amazing mystical things. The gods of that time called him "Vishnu," who had four arms and was the greatest god of all. The people of the village didn't care what others called him, they simply loved him because he was generous and kind. They called him Krishna, meaning "dark and beautiful."

One day, Krishna and his friends were tending their calves by the Yamuna River. "Here is a nice spot," he said. "The calves can drink from the river while we eat our lunch." The children sat on the ground and opened their baskets.

"Krishna," one child said, "look at my wonderful lunch." Krishna took a sweet from his friend's basket, popped it in his mouth, and all the children laughed. They were having so much fun that they did not see the calves wandering deep into the forest.

W hen the children finally looked up, the calves were gone. Were they in danger? "Krishna!" they cried out. "What should we do?!"

"Friends, " Krishna said, "continue with your lunch. I will find the calves." Off he went into the forest.

Brahma, chief of the gods, sat on his flying swan and watched. He had been hearing a lot about Krishna and was curious. "Why do the other gods think he is Vishnu, the greatest god of all? He is just a little boy," Brahma thought. He wanted to find out, so he stole the calves and put them to sleep in a mountain cave.

Krishna looked everywhere for the calves and went deeper into the forest. Meanwhile, Brahma went to the Yamuna River. He put the children to sleep, gathered them up, and hid them next to the sleeping calves in the mountain cave.

After a while, Krishna gave up looking for the calves and went back to the river. Now his friends were gone, too! "I can't return home alone," he thought. "The mothers and cows will be heartbroken without their children."

*K*rishna could not bear to be without his friends or bear the thought of how they would be missed. So he used his mystical powers to become a copy of each child and calf—for he was indeed four-armed Vishnu and dwelled in the hearts of all.

Each new child was perfect. Each wore the same clothing and ornaments as the child asleep in the cave. Each new calf was also perfect. The new calves were the same size and shape as the ones asleep in the cave—no two were alike.

Krishna copied each one in every detail. Their mothers would never know the difference, and their hearts would not be broken.

The children and calves entered the village of Vrindavan. As they did every day, the cowherd women came out to greet them. How wonderful their children looked! How much they reminded their mothers of darling Krishna. Love for their children mixed with their love for Krishna, and they smiled with joy.

After a while, Krishna and his friends walked on with their calves, looking for the cows and cowherd men who were off in the fields.

The cows were grazing on a hillside. When they saw their calves, they rushed down the hill before the cowherd men could stop them. The cows licked their calves with great affection.

At first the cowherd men were angry and ashamed, for they could not stop the cows from running away. But then they looked at their children and love for their children blended with their love for Krishna. The cowherd men embraced their children and forgot all anger and shame.

One year passed. Brahma returned to see
the mischief he had caused by stealing the
children and calves. When he reached Vrindavan,
he stopped and stared.

"What is this?" he wondered. "How did the
children and calves escape from the mountain
cave? I'm sure I put them to sleep. How are
they here again, playing with Krishna? Is this a
different group of children and calves?" Brahma,
the all-knowing chief of the gods, was confused.

*K*rishna wanted Brahma to know that such tricks were not a good idea. So from within each child and calf he appeared as four-armed Vishnu in a dazzling light. Brahma turned away from the bright light. A moment later he looked again. The children and calves were gone. There stood child Krishna, holding a flower and smiling.

"Dear Krishna," Brahma said, "please excuse me for stealing your friends. The gods were calling you Vishnu. I was jealous and wanted to prove them wrong. I am sorry. Please go to the Yamuna River, and I will make things right again."

Brahma quickly returned to the cave. He carried the sleeping children and calves to the bank of the Yamuna. The children woke up alongside their calves. It was as if no time had passed at all.

"Krishna," the children cried, "you found our calves! Thank you. Well, come on then. Let's finish our lunch."

And so they did. Afterward, they all returned home where the cowherd men and women were waiting for them.

The mystery of the stolen calves happened when Krishna was five years old. Soon he reached his sixth birthday and had more adventures—so wonderful to tell they were worth telling another day, in another book.

A Note to Parents and Teachers

KRISHNA AND THE MYSTERY OF THE STOLEN CALVES is adapted from the Bhagavata Purana, a classic wisdom text from India. Many tales from the Puranas feature child Krishna and friends overcoming obstacles of one kind or another, often posed by monsters or gods. The satisfaction in finding creative ways to excel despite great odds provides a bridge that can lead today's young readers to an appreciation of what might otherwise seem foreign in this ancient Sanskrit story.

INSIGHT KIDS
A MANDALA BOOK
PO Box 3088
San Rafael, CA 94912
www.insighteditions.com

www.MANDALAEARTHEDITIONS.com
FOR WEB EXCLUSIVE CONTENT!

Visit the author at: www.atma.org
Find us on Facebook: www.facebook.com/InsightEditions
Follow us on Twitter: @insighteditions

Text copyright © 2012 Joshua M. Greene
Illustrations copyright © 2012 Dominique Amendola

All rights reserved. No part of this book may be reproduced in any form without written permission from the publisher.

Library of Congress Cataloging-in-Publication Data available.

ISBN: 978-1-60887-173-5

Insigh Editi... ... ... f... ...
tree u...ed in t... ... ...
renowne... hum... ...
and con...erting ...
Peace w...ll plan...
...here w...

Manufactured in China by Insight Editions

10 9 8 7 6 5 4 3 2 1

APR 2018

WITHDRAWN

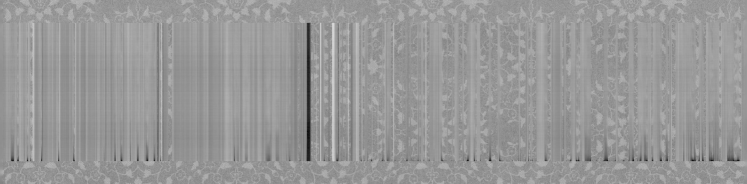